PURPOSE
IS A PACKAGE DEAL

Copyright © 2018 Courtney Riggins

Published by Godzchild Publications
a division of Godzchild, Inc.
22 Halleck St., Newark, NJ 07104
www.godzchildproductions.net

Printed in the United States of America 2018 - 1st Edition
Cover Design by Ana Esther of Es3lla Designs

All rights reserved. Except as permitted under the U.S. Copyright Act of 1976, this publication shall not be broadcast, rewritten, distributed, or transmitted, electronically or copied, in any form, or stored in a database or retrieval system, without prior written permission from the author.

Library of Congress Cataloging-in-Publications Data
Purpose Is A Package Deal/Courtney Riggins

ISBN   978-1-942705-53-6 (pbk)

1. Riggins, Courtney 2. Inspirational 3. Purpose 4. Faith
5. Self-Help 6. Christianity

2018

betrayal in my life. Letter by letter, the word spelled out PURPOSE.

To be honest, I had a hard time writing the beginning of this book. Hey, I told you in the beginning that this process wasn't easy! Granted the end and the middle were done, but for some odd reason I didn't have the words to say to start this journey; talk about frustrating! God has a funny way of doing things. One night as I was about to go to bed, I asked Him to give me the words to say to fill in the holes to this book, and then it hit me clear as day. He clearly said "Start with your story, the world isn't going to identify with you if they do not know your struggle." After my conversation with God that night, I figured that was the route that I needed to take. When I look back on everything that I have been through, I think my life can be summed up into one word: and that is PURPOSE.

As I reflect on my life, though I had difficult moments, I know for a fact now that God's hand was on me since the very moment I was born. I was the youngest of 5 kids on my mother's side and the oldest of 3 on my father's side. From what I was told, my birth mother had a lot on her plate including caring for a new baby, so with no other choice and for me to have my best chance to live a good life, she gave me up for adoption when I was 17 days old; that day, I went from being Ebone Lashay Clark, meaning "black" and

CHAPTER 1: **INTRODUCING ME**

It's been said that when we make plans, God totally laughs, and honestly, I think that's been the story of my life. God has His ways of speaking to us, and if we listen to what He's telling us it can be absolutely life changing. I had a dream once. I was in church and I saw that God was touching the lives of so many people. Everyone was worshipping and crying out to Him. The preacher asked everyone to line up so that she could give us something. She went on to explain that what she was about to give us was the one word that described the reason behind everything that we experienced in our lives. Everyone walked up one by one. Some began to cry, some fell to the floor, and others sighed in relief. It was finally my turn. At that point, it felt like my heart was beating out of my chest. I was so nervous! My palms were sweaty and I could barely catch my breath. I walked up and received my paper. I was a bit hesitant at first, but then I opened it slowly, and boom! There it was. Those bold, red letters, told me the reason why I went through so much hurt, stress, heartache and

PART 1: FINDING PURPOSE

He began to show me things that I still held on to. He revealed to me why I had to go through hard times and why I had to endure heartbreak and uncertainty, and He freed me from depression, fear and anxiety. God even rekindled and revamped some of the dreams I had inside of me that I thought had died. I realized that everything that I have ever faced in my life and the entire process led me to this moment: to encourage you, dear heart, with the words God gave me. Oftentimes we tell God, "Oh my gosh! Use me God! Send me to the nations! I'll be your willing vessel!" Trust me, I know, because I've said these things too, but can I be honest though? Most times we want to be used by God, but we have no idea what it takes to get there. Sometimes we don't want to go through the process to be developed for our "purpose" or "calling." Everything we face in our lives whether it be a heartbreak, addiction, even great times mold us and shape us into who God has called us to be. All of our experiences are a part of the package deal for our purpose. God has a plan for every one of us, but we must trust Him with it, yes even the hard times. My prayer for you, dear heart, is that as you read this book, the Lord will speak to you through each line, and that your life will change beyond measure just as mine was.

INTRO**DUCTION**

Ok, so if you're anything like me, I tend to skip the introductions to most books that I read, but let's not be like me on this occasion, promise? Can I be real with you? Writing this book was probably one of the hardest and most grueling things I have ever done in my life! The funny thing is, I didn't want to write it. It took God Himself to tell me to start writing. He told me that this book was going to change the lives of so many people and that I had to get the words out. So what did I do? I sat on it. I did nothing. Not because I didn't have the words to say, but because I was scared out of my mind! As God began to show me the things that He wanted me to write about, I flat out told Him no. Pretty bad, right? I didn't want people to know some of the things I struggled with.

Some people can be super judgmental and I didn't know what they would think of me after it was out. It took a lot of checking and a lot of getting over myself to begin to write. Then I realized through each chapter, God was doing a great work inside of my heart.

PART 3: WALKING IN PURPOSE WITH CONFIDENCE

CHAPTER 9
Staying Hydrated   [61]

CHAPTER 10
The Price of Purpose   [65]

CHAPTER 11
The Waiting Game   [71]

CHAPTER 12
Change Begins with You!   [75]

CHAPTER 13
Portion Control: The Danger of Comparison   [79]

CHAPTER 14
Fear Delays Your Future   [85]

CHAPTER 15
Deal or No Deal? Accepting the Offer   [91]

CONTENTS

Introduction   [1]

PART 1: FINDING PURPOSE

CHAPTER 1
Introducing Me   [5]

CHAPTER 2
Look Up! Purpose is Found in God   [15]

CHAPTER 3
Look Within and Look Ahead!   [21]

CHAPTER 4
Purpose is in Your Bloodline   [27]

PART 2: THE PROBLEMS THAT COME WITH PURPOSE

CHAPTER 5
Trusting God When You Don't Understand   [33]

CHAPTER 6
Growing Pains   [39]

CHAPTER 7
Divine Isolation and Separation   [43]

CHAPTER 8
It Comes with the Territory   [55]

Dedication

To my lifers: Dante' Barry, Jessica Barry and Steph Grace. We walked through the fire together and now we get to walk in the promise together. I love you guys so much!

"God's grace" to Courtney Renee Riggins, meaning "From the court" and "reborn". Isn't it amazing how God can do the same things with us? We are born into a world filled with dark, nasty sin and it is only through His grace that we can be reborn and have a real relationship with Him. If you are in Christ and have accepted Him as your Lord and Savior, then you have been adopted into a family of love and promise.

I guess you can say that I lived a pretty charmed life, a lot of people would say that I was spoiled. Hey, I'm not denying that! My adoptive family was wonderful; everything that I could ever want was at my fingertips. I took dance classes, was a cheerleader and I went to an exclusive private school. My family knew that there was something different about me and that I was born to do something out of the norm. I was smart and was given the world, but deep down I knew that something was missing.

In some cases, adoption can cause some to develop roots of abandonment and rejection which can cause some to act out in various ways to fill that place in their heart that they think is empty. In my case, I turned to people pleasing and seeking the approval of others. I took what others said about me as law. I had no sense of self at all. If someone called me stupid or ugly, I believed it. I didn't feel good about myself. Low self-esteem got the best of me so much so that when others would tell me I was pretty or smart, I didn't believe it. The mirror became one of my biggest enemies. I hated to look at myself. Sometimes I found myself angry with God and questioned Him about the way I looked. My need for attachment was out of control. I found myself falling into depression when people left my life for whatever reason. I took on the blame and convinced myself that if I were prettier, smarter and more fun to be around that they would have stayed. I longed to be accepted anywhere, and I tried to do anything I could to have someone to call a friend. I remember giving away my lunch money or some of my toys so that other kids would be nice to me. I lived for the acceptance of my peers. Granted, I loved my family, but there were times when I didn't feel completely apart. I was given everything, but there was still a void inside my heart. I was loved, but somehow I knew I was different. I was an only child adopted into a family where both of my parents were basically the only living children on their sides, so it felt as if I had no one to identify and connect with that was close to my age. With that strong desire to be accepted and willing to do anything to fit in came many years of verbal, mental and emotional abuse from my peers and even some adults. I attended a predominantly white private school for most of my childhood. Fitting in was rough. It felt as though I needed to own the right designer clothes and have a certain amount of money and spoke a certain way to be accepted. Sure, I was a cheerleader and sometimes hung out with the popular kids, but it still felt as if I were the lowest of the low. My hair wasn't straight enough and I wasn't skinny enough, so the idea of being asked out or wanted was pretty much nonexistent for me. Things seemed to get better the summer before I entered high school. I just made Varsity cheerleading and was nailing every routine and even started to make more friends. Things were looking up for me. I was excited about the new chapter I was about to start, and then it happened. Just as I got off the bus from cheerleading camp, my mom informed me and my coaches that I was transferring to another school. Talk about disappointment!

My world was rocked when I realized I was transferring from a predominately white private school to a predominately black public school on the opposite side of town. My parents tried to reassure me time and time again that the move was good for me, but I refused to listen. I'm grateful for it now, but back then I was livid! Talk about a culture shock! My first day of high school was a pretty interesting one. People would look at me strange when I stood up during class and introduced myself. People were shocked every time I opened my mouth and I didn't understand why. It wasn't until lunchtime when I was talking to a few kids I met during the day and one of them said to me, "You know, you're *really* white. Where are you from?" and another chimed in, "You know you're black, right? You gotta act like it."

> *Huh? What are you talking about?*
> *This is how I've always been!*
> *This is me!*

I found myself in the same position as I was before: doing everything I could to fit in. I listened to certain music and tried to talk a certain way and I changed my hair and my style countless times and it still didn't work! I still stuck out like a sore thumb. Some people dubbed me as the white girl who was stuck up and better than everyone else, while others thought I was a sellout and brainwashed. It got to a point where I didn't even want to talk anymore. At one point, I failed my classes on purpose hoping that my parents would reenroll me in my previous school. Let me tell you, that plan failed *miserably.* It appeared that I never got a break. Even certain family members would mock me and criticize me because they thought I was better than them. It bothered them that I was doing well in school and it was clear that I had a bright future ahead of me. Had I known that the reason behind their ridicule was because I had a higher calling on my life and that God had set me apart, I would have handled things differently. Even then it wasn't enough. If the ridicule wasn't happening in my own family and at school, it was happening at church of all places. Now, you would think the church would be safe, right? I've come to realize through several experiences that church hurt is a real thing and if left unaddressed and unhealed, it can cause detrimental effects not only to a person's emotional and mental wellbeing, but it can be a huge blow to a person's walk with Jesus.

Part of me has always had a desire and hunger for God and I wanted to know more about Him. I would get so excited about learning about who He was to me and discovering new things in the Bible. *(fun fact: when I was 8 years old I recited the 10 commandments instead of reciting an Easter speech like the rest of the kids…who does that?)* Some of the kids in my youth group and even some of the adults in my church didn't seem to share in my excitement. Anytime they saw me praying or engaging during our services and lessons they would always have something hurtful to say. I would hear some of the other kids giggling because I sang and lifted my hands during worship. Some were petty and spread rumors about me throughout our youth group that clearly weren't true. I can remember a time where I was a part of the dance ministry at my church.

People would tell me that they would be blessed and inspired when I dance, but on one occasion during practice, a grown lady, emphasis on grown, came up to me and told me that I wasn't graceful enough and walked away; again, seriously, who does that? People often took advantage of me because I was the "good girl" and because I wanted to do the right thing by showing them the love of Christ. I realized that after so many years of giving everything that I had for sake of having someone to talk to, that some people just didn't want to be my friend. Some completely forgot about me as an individual and only wanted what I could give them. Part of me knew I was more than that. As I began to mature, I grew tired of being controlled and manipulated all the time, but sadly, I didn't know what to do about it, so I kept my mouth shut. Some people knew that I wouldn't say anything when they offended or criticized me without any reason at all. They knew I would keep quiet when they touched me inappropriately and invaded my space and made fun of me and told people that I had sex inside of the church. They knew I was the "goody two shoes" and that I needed to know my place. It got to the point where I never felt like I was enough. I wasn't good enough, I wasn't pretty enough, I wasn't "black or white" enough, I wasn't rich enough. I never had the right designer clothes, or right designer shoes. I never had the right hair or the right style, and

CHAPTER 1: INTRODUCING ME

the list goes on. I found myself completely depressed and defeated. I felt like I didn't have a voice. It felt like I was screaming but no one could hear me, and unfortunately, this cycle continued for most of my teen years.

I moved to Tampa to attend college, and to be honest with you, moving was the most liberating thing I did. Being away from the people and situations that hurt me the most, I began to find myself and venture out. Though I grew up in church and went to a Christian school, there were seasons in my life where I was angry with God. I felt that He was the reason behind all my pain. I knew about Him and even read my Bible, but I thought to myself, if He was God and He loved me, why would He let these things happen? I felt that since He let certain things happen in my life, I was going to do my own thing. It was time to finally do things my way for once. I was on a mission to rid myself of that good girl image once and for all. I went to parties, went to a few clubs every now and then. Popped any kind of pills I could find just for the rush. The people that I associated with were nice and didn't mind that I did those things at all, but somehow they knew that I didn't belong. Come to think of it, I knew that I didn't belong, but I didn't care. I still wanted to drink. I still wanted to watch stuff that I had no business watching. I still wanted to do me, but my heart was still aching for something more. I needed God. I just knew it.

At one point, it felt like everything was weighing down on me at once and that I had come to the end of myself. I couldn't stand it anymore. I told God to give me a way out or else I would die. Looking ahead, God led me to a wonderful ministry on my campus that helped guide me back to what was important. To be honest, it felt like home. Over time I learned that God had a plan and a purpose just for me, and that everything that happened in my life was for His will and my greater good. I thought to myself: *"Wait, what? Plans? What purpose? Me? I really don't have anything to offer; plus, nobody knows me, heck, I hardly even know myself!"* As I grew deeper in God, He led me to pursue my passions, those things that I dreamed of doing my entire life, but never got the chance to. He began breaking down the walls I had placed around my heart and He freed me from my hurt. It was in this season where I began to discover my purpose.

CHAPTER 2: **LOOK UP!** PURPOSE IS FOUND IN GOD

Finding your purpose in God must come from God Himself. This means getting to know Him is number 1. God is the creator of all things; He knows each and every being and what they were created to do. Finding purpose means to find God. The only way we are going to know the true function and capability of a product is to go to the manufacturer Himself. In other words, to find purpose, we must get on our faces and seek Him with all our heart. Now, let me share something. Seeking God doesn't mean going to Him and saying "okay God, I want to do this, and I want to do it the way I planned. I've told you about it and I know you're going to bless me." Promise me you won't be that person. Trust me, it's not a fun place to be.

    I remember a time where I thought seeking God meant just telling Him what I wanted to do, telling Him what He was going to do, and then going out and doing those things I wanted to do and eventually falling flat on my face and getting angry with Him because I thought I "sought" Him and got His blessing in the first place. I remember when I wanted to start a nonprofit organization for girls. Sure, I had a business plan. I had goals and events. I had it all lined up, but it seemed like every time I would step forward to do something, it would fall apart. Sure, people came and it was a lot of fun, but at the end of the day, I was left with little to no money, no energy and nowhere to go next. I remember asking God why in the world was this happening. I mean, I thought He gave me the vision and I stepped out on faith. Why wasn't it working out? In the midst of my frustration I heard God say "I never told you to do any of that stuff, and you never asked me what to do in the first place. Your plans will only get you so far and doing it in your own strength is silly. You need me." You can bet that I straightened up after that! When I finally surrendered my plans and goals to the Lord, He downloaded what He wanted me to do and the steps I should take. Jeremiah 29:12 tells us that if we will seek Him with all of our hearts, we will find Him. That means in the same way we stop everything that we're doing to find our lost car keys or our misplaced iPhone (I'm an Apple girl, ya'll) is the same way we need to seek after

CHAPTER 2: LOOK UP! PURPOSE IS FOUND IN GOD

Christ. Seeking God requires faith: that unshakeable, indescribable belief that something or someone exists. Seeking God requires us to realize that no matter what happens, God is always there, even when we can't see Him, feel Him, or hear Him. He is there, after all, He is an omnipresent God. Hebrews 11:6 tells us that without faith it is impossible to please God, and when we come to Him we must have faith and know who He is and that He will reward us if we seek Him diligently. What am I saying here? I'm asking you, my friend, to look inside of yourself and ask, how bad do I want it? How bad do I want to change the world and others around me? How badly do I want to hear God's voice? How badly do I want to get to my "something bigger" and "something more"? It all starts at the source, and that is God. As we seek Him and get to know who He is, He begins to show us who we are. We begin to understand His character and His attributes and slowly but surely, God makes us into who we were called to be. Start from the source, get to know God, and get to know yourself.

REFLECTION

1. Who is God to you? List 3 things that you know about God. I know for me when I started my relationship with Christ, He was a friend, a restorer and healer. Who has He been to you?

_____

_____

_____

2. Find 3 more characteristics of God in the Bible. Doing this will help you get into the habit of studying the Word and getting to know Him more. For example, Psalm 23:1 tells us that He is a shepherd. 1 John 4:8 tells us that God is love.

_____

_____

_____

3. What does God say about you? Dwell on the following scriptures and really think about how God views you and what He wants to do through you,

*Before I formed you in the womb I knew you, before you were born I set you apart; I appointed you as a prophet to the nations." -**Jeremiah 1:5***

*For I know the plans I have for you," declares the Lord, "plans to prosper you and not to harm you, plans to give you hope and a future. -**Jeremiah 29:11***

*For you created my inmost being, you knit me together in my mother's womb. I praise you because I am fearfully and wonderfully made; your works are wonderful; I know that full well. - **Psalm 139:13-14***

*But you are a chosen people, a royal priesthood, a holy nation, God's special possession, that you may declare the praises of him who called you out of darkness into his wonderful light. -**1 Peter 2:9***

_____

_____

_____

_____

_____

CHAPTER 3: **LOOK WITHIN AND LOOK AHEAD!**

What do you like to do? What drives you? What makes you absolutely mad? Look within yourself because what you're passionate about is a key indicator of what you have been called to do. The very thing that upsets you could be the very thing you were designed to change. It's been said that purpose can be found in our greatest pain. Oftentimes we are called and assigned to the place that caused us our greatest misery. Moses, for example, had a heart for the people of Israel. He hated to see people being treated unfairly. Moses even killed a guard who was beating a slave. Before Moses' actions were discovered, he ran away, leaving behind everything that he knew and loved. As he was in the desert doing what he thought was the right thing at the time, God called him back to the place of oppression, back to the place where his heart grieved but wasn't sure why, back to the place where he called home.

Thinking back to when God gave me the vision

for Raise Your Voice Inc., a ministry that helps people find their voice and identity in Christ, I always had the desire to work with kids and to help people. He told me to write down what angered me, what makes me miserable, and everything I would say to people if I got the chance. That's when it hit me, not having a voice absolutely angers me, and I feel that everyone should have their say in what they feel is important to them. I absolutely hate bullies and it pains me to see people taken advantage of. It annoys me to see people live the opposite of who they were called to be. I think it's so funny how God works. Just thinking about my journey, it hasn't been an easy road. Heck, it still isn't easy. It's been a process. I'll tell you the truth and say that finding God's purpose for your life is not going to be easy. It can be hard at times! Especially if you find yourself lost and going in circles.

When I first started college I was a pre-med major, thinking to myself that I was going to become a pediatric neurosurgeon that was going to save the lives of millions of kids (ambitious much?). I thought I could do it. I was smart. I took all honors courses in high school and aced them with flying colors. I thought it was perfect...until I enrolled in Chemistry and Calculus. It was so hard! I failed every assignment and every test. I got so discouraged that I changed my major to political science, thinking to myself that since pre-med didn't work out, so why not be a family lawyer and child advocate? I'll still be able to help people. With 2 years of school behind me and a bachelor's degree under my belt, I decided to give pre-med one more try, and to my surprise, I failed the SAME classes again! I didn't know what to do at that point. I kept saying, God, you know I want to be somebody, but what am I supposed to do? What about my plans? I keep failing! Not too long after, I found myself at a restaurant with a friend of mine. She asked me what I wanted to do in life. I told her that I wanted to work with kids and make a difference in the lives of people, but I keep failing my classes and all my efforts seem like they are going to waste. Her response to my statement changed my life forever: "So why are you taking this route again? It's getting you nowhere." Everything changed for me after that. I changed my major to Psychology and breezed through it, and was offered a job as a social worker for abused and neglected kids immediately after graduation.

    I said all that to say this: when you allow yourself to be led by God, and not your own motives and will, He will lead you where you need to go. So I'm asking you, what is it that gets you going? I encourage you to take some time and reflect. Take this time to let God heal you from all of your past hurts. Take this time to let go of your will and truly allow God to lead and guide you. In order to be used mightily by God, you must first be broken deeply by God. The things you go through in this life aren't all about you. Your story can help change and restore so many people if you choose to deal with those hard times properly.

Looking back at my own life, I always wondered why I had to be adopted. Why couldn't I just be born into my adoptive family? Somehow I thought it would make things easier for me. Surprisingly God revealed to me that there were several generational curses and strongholds in my bloodline. Adoption was in His plan for me in order for those curses and strongholds to be broken. I'll never forget what He told me. He said "the curses and strongholds that have been passed on from generation to generation stop with you. I have called you to break them so that you can help other people break theirs as well." There was a certain path God needed me on, and I realized that He used my birth parents as the vessels to bring me in to the world. This life, our struggles, the things that we go through are seriously so much bigger than what we think and perceive. We must process them in a healthy way so that we can become stronger and better. Whether it be through counseling, writing, praying and pouring out to Him, do what you need to do in order to overcome that hurdle. Don't sit and wallow in your hurt and pain, because it will eventually overtake you. Choose to heal healthily because the world is waiting to hear your story.

REFLECTION

1. What are some things that you enjoy doing? What are some things that you are passionate about?

_____

_____

_____

_____

2. What are some things that you need to let go of and heal from? Ask God to show you anything inside of you that needs to be corrected and that needs to be healed. And as you reflect in your quiet time, dwell on Ephesians 4:22-24

> *Throw off your old sinful nature and your former way of life, which is corrupted by lust*

and deception. Instead, let the Spirit renew your thoughts and attitudes. Put on your new nature, created to be like God—truly righteous and holy.

CHAPTER 4: **PURPOSE IS IN YOUR BLOODLINE!**

I'll tell you the truth and say that discovering purpose is absolutely not easy, and following it will not be a walk in the park. I absolutely love The Princess Diaries. Those close to me know that I've seen it a million times. The amazing thing is that I never realized how strong of a message the movie had regarding purpose.

To make a long movie short, Mia was completely invisible to everyone. She appeared to be the laughing stock of her entire class. Her looks and appearance didn't appeal to anyone. She was afraid to speak in front of people; she even threw up when she was called to speak. She was the queen of clumsy and lacked all kinds of grace. But one day, something happened; she was summoned by her grandmother, Queen of Genovia. Her grandmother explained to Mia that her father, who recently passed away, was a prince, making Mia a princess. Mia was completely baffled, asking over and over how in the world she could be a princess. She wasn't pretty enough nor did she have the authority to rule over anyone, or as she would say, "she was no princess, she was still waiting for normal body parts to arrive". Her grandmother wasn't having any of that and wasn't taking any of Mia's excuses. She explained that royalty was in Mia's bloodline, and that she was the only heir to the throne. If she did not rule, the kingdom of Genovia would eventually crumble. To bring it home, we are never qualified for the call on our lives. Though some may be called to preach and speak to the nations, they may be the shyest, clumsiest and most reserved people ever. If someone were to tell me 10 years ago that I was called to preach and help people all over the world, I would have told them that they were lying! Just a little confession: I can be a little reserved sometimes, but we'll talk more about that later. Often times, who we are as individuals tend to be the opposite of who we are called to be. 1 Corinthians 1:26-31 tells us that God doesn't call the qualified, He qualifies the called.

> ***26 Brothers and sisters, think of what you were when you were called. Not many of you were wise by human standards; not many were influential; not many were of noble birth. 27 But God chose the foolish things of the world to shame the wise; God chose the weak things of the world to shame the strong. 28 God chose the lowly things of this world and the despised***

> *things—and the things that are not—to nullify the things that are, 29 so that no one may boast before him. 30 It is because of him that you are in Christ Jesus, who has become for us wisdom from God—that is, our righteousness, holiness and redemption. 31 Therefore, as it is written: "Let the one who boasts boast in the Lord."*

Overtime, Mia received the proper training through reading, speaking, etc. Mia was even made over physically. Mia had to become relatable, sociable, and knowledgeable enough to fulfill her calling as princess. Through many tests and trials Mia was going to abdicate her call as princess. After much thought and soul searching, Mia accepted and received her call in confidence. Say it with me: Purpose is in my bloodline. You are called to make a difference. Through proper training and development you WILL become that great person that God has created you to be. Purpose is not a probability, but a mandate. Your training is not an option, it is a requirement. Are you ready?

PART 2:
THE PROBLEMS THAT COME

CHAPTER 5: **TRUSTING GOD WHEN YOU DON'T UNDERSTAND**

Maybe God promised you something and you haven't seen the fruit of that promise yet. Maybe you've had a loved one pass away and you don't understand how or why. Maybe you just had a bad breakup. Whatever it is, I encourage you to put your trust in the Lord. He's the one who sees you and knows exactly where you are. I've had some pretty trying times in my life, especially in these past couple of years. I've experienced everything from loss, to church hurt and even betrayal to the extreme from people I thought were always going to be in my corner. I had so much anger and confusion inside of me. Oftentimes I would question why God would let certain things happen to me. Why did I have to leave that church? Why didn't anyone have my back or at least call me to see if I was ok? Why in the world are people I don't even talk to spreading rumors about me and why are the people I thought were the closest to me believing them? These are questions I had to ask.

It wasn't easy and I didn't understand. It felt like one moment I was on top of the world serving and giving my all in the church and so many people were there cheering me on and the next I'm the lowest of the low.

After I parted ways with my previous church, it felt as if I had no sense of identity anymore. It felt as though my entire life and my entire world was consumed with doing and trying to look a certain way all to get the stamp of approval from man. I didn't know who I was anymore, and I doubted that I had purpose. There were times where I was so discouraged that I believed the lies of the enemy that told me that God wasn't even for me. I found myself at the point of wanting to give up and end it all. There were days where I didn't even want to get out of bed. Depression, anxiety and defeat had strong holds on me. There were days where I didn't even want to pray, and when I did try to pray I couldn't even muster up the words to express how I felt. There days where I didn't even see the point in living for God if He was going to bring so much pain in my life. I felt like I was going through so much hell and nothing was getting better. It felt like I was in the deepest pit and couldn't find my way out, but it was when I truly relied on Jesus and gave Him all my cares and all my worries that I began to see the light at the end of the tunnel. It was when I was honest and open with Him that He helped me through the hard times, and He continues to

CHAPTER 5: TRUSTING GOD WHEN YOU DON'T UNDERSTAND

be right there by my side. Some days are better than others if I can be honest. Some days my emotions and circumstances still try to get the best of me, but it's in those moments where I know I need to lean on the Lord.

I just wanted to encourage you dear heart, that even when it feels like you're in your darkest moments, Jesus is right there with you. Psalm 139 tells us that we can never escape His presence. Darkness and light are the same to Him. He sees us in our high moments and our lowest moments.

- To the one who is in a predicament that you don't quite understand and that you don't want to be in.
- To the one who is waiting for something to shake in their life.
- To the one who has been trusting and believing God to come through and haven't quite seen results yet.
- To the one who feels like they don't have the strength to pray.

I encourage you to stand firm.

Some things we go through aren't meant for us to understand, but they are meant to build our trust and faith in the Lord. How would we ever know God as a healer if we never experience sickness or hurt? How would we ever know Him as restorer if we never had our heart broken or faced disappointment? How would we ever know Him as faithful if our backs were never against the wall and we had nowhere to turn? To be honest, I may never fully understand why certain people left and why they hurt me the way they did, but I can say this: God used that time in my life to build me and to make me stronger. He led me to another church and brought amazing leaders in my life to help push and grow me. It may sound a little cliché, but God broke me down just to build me back up again. He changed my mindset. He taught me how to forgive and to love, and He sweetly reminded me that what He called me to do was far greater than I could ever imagine. I want to encourage you dear heart. In those moments where it feels like you have nowhere to turn, look up, for that is where your help is found. Let's look at Psalm 121:

I lift up my eyes to the mountains—
where does my help come from?
My help comes from the Lord,
the Maker of heaven and earth.
He will not let your foot slip—
he who watches over you will not slumber;
indeed, he who watches over Israel
will neither slumber nor sleep.
The Lord watches over you—
the Lord is your shade at your right hand;
the sun will not harm you by day,

> *nor the moon by night.*
> *The Lord will keep you from all harm—*
> *he will watch over your life;*
> *the Lord will watch over your coming and going*
> *both now and forevermore.*

You see, our help and our hope is found in God alone. My prayer for you is that you continue to fix your eyes on the One who sees all and knows all about you, and that you find your strength in Him. Granted, you may still have issues and things may still happen; bills still need to get paid and people may still get on your nerves. You may not still understand, but as you continue to trust God and spend time with Him, He'll give you a different perspective and will show you how to walk through it. It continues to work for me, and I know it will work for you!

CHAPTER 6: **GROWING PAINS**

How often have we asked God to use us and to make us look more like Him, and when situations occur in our lives that seem too hard or too impossible to endure that we completely run away or quit? I know I've been there. As I've shared with you, it hasn't been easy. There have been days where I had to fake it. I painted a smile on my face in front of others, but behind closed doors I was an absolute mess. I cried, I kicked and I screamed. There was even a time where I got so angry that I repeatedly kicked my door. Hey, I could have kicked it down if I wanted to. To be honest with you, I wanted to quit on the whole God thing. Nothing was working out the way they I hoped. I was still single with no prospects in sight. I barely had any friends. There were still some people who were against me. It felt like things were going downhill for me. Have you been there? I know things may be a little tough right now, but maybe, just maybe God is using this time to grow you.

We must be mindful of what we pray and ask

God for because He most certainly hears us! If you ask Him to make you look more like Him and to make you better, then of course tests are going to come your way. There are going to be times where someone comes and tells you about yourself and shed some light on issues in your heart that you've hidden away for years. There was a time not too long ago when I asked God to show me anything that I was missing and to show me anything that I needed to work on. No lie, the very next day God used a close friend of mine to shed light on issues that I've held onto for years. I was shocked because I thought I already overcame it. I found myself discouraged because it felt like I hadn't grown as much as I thought, but God quickly reminded me that if I continued to submit to Him and not rush the process, that it would be a little easier. Dear heart, I just wanted to encourage you to keep going and don't give up. The tough times you're facing are only temporary. Endure these growing pains! You will come out stronger and better if you endure. Let's look at James 1:2-4:

Dear brothers and sisters, when troubles of any kind come your way, consider it an opportunity for great joy. 3 For you know that when your faith is tested, your endurance has a chance to grow. 4 So let it grow, for when your endurance is fully developed, you will be perfect and complete, needing nothing.

CHAPTER 6: GROWING PAINS

You see, hard times come to make us stronger. They come to mature us and to help us develop the character of Jesus. Yes, it may be hard right now, but just think how else would you develop patience if people didn't get on your nerves? Trust me, I know this to be a fact! How else would you develop love if people never talked about you behind your back and yet you didn't choose to be petty or spiteful towards them? How else would you develop the fruit of the spirit if you weren't placed in tough situations? Want to know if you're growing and producing fruit? Look at your life and things around you. Are the things that normally bother and annoy you affect you as much? Are you finding yourself handling that difficult person a little better? Congratulations! You're growing, but don't stop there. Keep going! There was a season in my life where God needed me to rely on only Him. I had so many distractions in front of me. I gave people more attention than I did God, so what did He do? He stripped me from everything and everyone that I placed higher than Him. It hurt. I didn't understand at times. I was so angry at God because I thought that He didn't want me to be happy. After numerous pouting and crying sessions, He sweetly reminded me that because of the purpose He had for my life, I needed to learn total dependence on Him. Do I have it all together now? Ha!

Yeah, right! I still have my moments every now and then, but I'm finding myself getting stronger and closer to God.

Dear heart, it may be tough right now, but these are the moments where you must cling to The Lord. You must get in the word of God and feed on it and pray like your life depends on it, because it does. You must submit your feelings and emotions to the Lord. Be honest with Him about how you're feeling and ask Him for help, and He'll come through for you! Believe it or not, He loves to help His children! God doesn't want us to try to figure out life all on our own, but He wants to do life with us His way. The right way. Be encouraged and know that though you may be going through tough times, it's the perfect opportunity for you to grow closer to Jesus.

CHAPTER 7: **DIVINE ISOLATION AND SEPARATION**

Is it just me, or does everyone seem to have haters these days? For the ones that are unaware of this phenomenon, a hater is someone who becomes envious of your success or simply will not be happy until you hit rock bottom. One of the key realizations that come with discovering and walking in your purpose is the fact that people will not always be in your corner. Let's be real, when you go against what people expect you to do, you're going to have some opposition. With that opposition comes the fact that some people will not hang around; it all boils down to one thing when fulfilling your purpose: those around you must get with it or get lost.

I think one of the biggest people other than Jesus that dealt with haters was Joseph. God promised Joseph that he would be a great leader, even his own brothers would bow down to him. However, before that even came to past, he would have to face betrayal, isolation and loss. When Joseph told his brothers everything that

God showed him, his brothers became furious. They did not want to see Joseph succeed at all, so much so that they sold him as a slave. Here's a little nugget: Not everyone is meant to know what God has called you to do and what He is doing through you. Use wisdom and don't share it with the world! God will place people in your life that will recognize and help cultivate what's in you. There's no need to go telling it to the mountaintops. The enemy has ears too, and he will do everything in his power to stop the plan of God for your life. *Steps down from soapbox* As the story goes on, Joseph was betrayed, lied on, forgotten about, and it seemed that all was lost for him. Through it all, it was in those situations where he was eventually elevated into His purpose as ruler over all of Egypt. How did Joseph deal with the problems that came with his purpose? He served and trusted God wholeheartedly. His situation was unfortunate but necessary as they placed him into the position he needed to be to save the people and to be reunited with his family. It was in Joseph's times of isolation and separation that God did his best work.

    Let's face it, we all want people in our corner, and it can be extremely painful and sometimes depressing when we feel that we are fighting this fight all by ourselves. I'm going to be real with you, oftentimes I would ask God why He wouldn't allow me to get close to certain people. At times I would find myself completely depressed because I felt that I couldn't click with people. I always felt that the moment I would reach a certain level of intimacy with someone, they would leave in some way or another. Growing up, I always had the mindset of "people always leave." Granted, that was something that stemmed from being adopted and dealing with feelings of rejection and abandonment. One day God showed me how relationships operate in the form of rooms in house and where everyone in our lives fit in.

Living Room: Our house represents our inner circle, that inner space in which people dwell. We have a living room, where almost all guest are welcomed. The living room is usually the most open space in the home. Sure, it's big, but it's comfortable just enough for guests to stay only for a little while. Most social gatherings happen in this space, and they are often the place for ice breakers and introductions. Acquaintances and people that we aren't as intimate with fall into the area of living room guests.

Kitchen: The kitchen is open but is a bit more intimate. I love to cook, and I love my kitchen. Not everyone has the privilege of just walking in my kitchen, going through my cabinets and refrigerator taking and using anything that they please; that just doesn't go down in my house. I have a rule in my house that if you are a first time guest, I am more than happy to go in the kitchen for you to get a drink or snack, but if you've been in my house more than 3 times or if you are a frequent visitor, you know where to find something to drink if you're thirsty. Are you hungry? You know where the refrigerator and snacks are, help yourself. You don't allow anyone in the kitchen; it requires a deeper relationship than the regular living room guest. Those with kitchen access have some sort of influence in your life. These guests have the ability to nurture you physically, emotionally and spiritually. Bonding moments happen in the kitchen. Magic can happen in the kitchen. You wouldn't want to make magic with just anyone, would you? And granted you wouldn't want to eat everyone's cooking. It takes a deeper level of trust to be invited in the kitchen in order to bring together something that will help strengthen me and make me a little healthier and happier.

Bedrooms: Finally, we have the actual rooms. This type of access is only granted to those who are nearest and dearest to us: best friends, husband, wife, children, parents, etc. These rooms hold different levels of intimacy. The master bedroom contains the intimacy of a husband and wife. I'm not married, but I have married friends. One of my closest friends is a newlywed, and one afternoon we were at her house just talking and enjoying each other's company when she asked me

CHAPTER 7: DIVINE ISOLATION AND SEPARATION

to come in her room for a minute as she freshened up. As I stepped into the room, I thought to myself, "This room isn't the same anymore, the same bed we had sleepovers and countless girl talks now houses a husband and a wife." I have this thing where I dare not even think about looking in a married couple's room. To me, it is a sanctuary and very sacred. (I could go on and on about this, but that's definitely for another time.) Bedrooms contain relationship between parent and children, mother and daughter, father and son, etc.

I said all that to say this: some people may be in your space, but they may not be called to have a place in your heart. Unfortunately, not everyone will support what God has called you to do, and the ones you that you think should be there probably won't be. There are times where God separates us from the ones we hold dear, whether it is a friend, boyfriend/girlfriend, or family member. Don't feel bad, it's not you, it's not them, it's your CALLING. Divine separation allows us to move closer to God. I know many times in my life where God removed almost everyone in my circle. Sure, it didn't feel good, and yes, I kicked and screamed that nobody loved me, nobody was there for me and that I was all alone. Heck, I even went through a season where nobody called and barely texted me for almost a year. I would wonder what even the point of having a phone was. These past couple of years have been trying for me especially when it came to my relationships. I noticed that slowly but surely God removed people that were unnecessary out of my life. Sure, I considered them to be my best friends at the time, but they were crutches for me. When I felt lonely, I would go and hang out with them. When I needed advice, they would be the first ones I would call. When I needed affirmation, they gave it to me. To be honest, God wasn't even in the forefront of my mind. I didn't think to turn to Him for what I needed because I always had people around that did that, but oh how He shifted things in my life! I found myself working from home and being by myself for about 12 hours out of my day. Think about it. There are 24 hours in a day, about 12 of them were by myself, about 8 of the them were for sleeping, and I would have a few hours left for just a little social interaction…. MAYBE, depending on the day and depending on people's schedules. It was so hard for me.

I kept telling God that being by myself most of the time couldn't be healthy for me and that I needed people. There were some days where I got super angry with God. I would tell him how I was angry that he removed so many people out of my life and how I was just stuck there with nowhere and no one to turn to. It just felt so dry and so quiet around me, and some days, the silence drove me crazy. I would LOATHE being at

CHAPTER 7: DIVINE ISOLATION AND SEPARATION

home by myself. Eventually I realized that it is through those times where God speaks to us the most. If you allow it to be, your most silent moments can be the loudest moments, and your weakest moments can be your strongest moments. 2 Corinthians 12:9 tells us that God's strength is made perfect in our weakness. God began to speak to me even in the middle of my frustrations and pity parties. He told me that I would never know Him as a friend, as a provider, as a protector if I never went through these seasons. God was using that season of my life to draw me closer to Him.

A couple of years ago I suffered a dislocated kneecap and a torn ligament from dancing which led to relying on crutches for 2 months and caused me to sit out from basically everything that I was involved in. Let me tell you something, I was embarrassed and hurt, but I think my ego was hurting more than my leg. Me? Sit and do nothing? Please, I'm always doing something. That was my problem. I was always doing something. Sure I had a relationship with God, but it wasn't where it needed to be, especially during that time as I was in the process of becoming a minister. God needed me to Himself; there were still some things that He needed to strip me from. I kicked, I screamed, I pouted and got angry with God because I thought I was in my prime, I needed to be active, I need to be a busybody, after all, I'm doing His work. I got to a place of discouragement and felt like I wasn't as effective as I used to be in ministry because I was "doing nothing". Oh how my mind was so twisted back then! I look back and I thank God for that time because I'm definitely not the same person I was. My relationship with God has become stronger than ever, and I am so grateful that He loved me that much to want me all to Himself.

So what do you do in those moments of isolation and silence? Pray consistently. There was a point in my life when I didn't even know how to pray. I figured that if I wasn't on my knees or if my face wasn't buried in the ground all the while throwing in the occasional "thee, thou or thine" or calling down fire from Heaven that I wasn't praying right. Just talk to Him! Talking to God isn't rocket science, just pour your heart out to Him. To be honest with you, there were times where my heart felt so broken that my mouth couldn't even form the words to even say to God I'm so grateful for His spirit that lives inside of us as believers. Romans 8:26-27 tells us that when we don't know what to pray, the Holy Spirit intercedes for us. Even a simple sigh or groan means everything to the Lord; He most certainly understands it! There would be times where I would just sit on my floor and cry. I would be completely speechless. Thankfully God knows what our tears mean. He collects all of them and records them. (That's Psalm 56:8, one of my favorite scriptures!)

CHAPTER 7: DIVINE ISOLATION AND SEPARATION

Seasons of separation and isolation are a call back to Him. It was in this season, and I noticed that I tend to go through this season in cycles, that I grew closer to God and became stronger and more confident in who He created me to be. I got to know Him more. I grew to know more of His likes and His dislikes, and when I would pray and spend time with Him, I could literally feel Him come into the room. That doesn't just happen automatically, it takes relationship and that one on one time with the Lord.

Pay attention! God has a word concerning you. Place your cares, desires, and feelings on Him. Pour out to God; He wants to hear from you. Divine separation isn't comfortable and it definitely isn't easy. When it is all said and done, you can look back and know that you were never truly alone. In those isolated moments, you'll realize that God was with you during those nights where you cried yourself to sleep and felt like giving up. For those that know me well, you know that I struggled with depression and self-harm for many seasons of my life. It got to the point where it felt like no one was there and no one loved me, and if I were never here, the world wouldn't miss me. I believed the lies of the enemy that told me that I was just a waste of space and I didn't matter and that God had no plans for me life. It was absolutely tormenting. I hated myself for it, so much to the point that I wanted to end it all. It was God who kept me from using that knife and taking those pills. I heard His voice so clearly that day, "If you only knew how much I loved you, and how much I had in store for you. You were never alone. Come back to your first love." Those life changing words in my season of despair led me to His Word, my daily bread. Over time I began to learn of His unfailing love for me and that He truly had something great in mind when He made me. Do I still go through seasons where I'm feeling isolated and separated? Absolutely! But I've grown to learn that I am never truly alone in those times. Instead of listening to those voices that make me feel horrible about myself and that makes me want to curse the season that I'm in, I've learned how to fight back with the truth, which is God's word. Honestly guys, it's in these kind of seasons where God tends to strengthen you the most....if you let Him. You have to push past your flesh and the thoughts that try to flood your mind and truly rely on God. Pray, get rid of everything that is distracting you and truly embrace what He is trying to do in your heart during these times. God is there, and He is definitely in your corner. Though it may not feel like it at times, there is truly beauty in these kind of seasons! Thank God for your isolated and quiet moments, because He wants to speak to you, hear from you and pour into you something oh so great!

REFLECTION

1. Alone time with God is very important to our growth. Just look at Jesus! He was healing the sick and helping so many people, and yet He still needed to get away every now and then to reconnect with His Father. Staying connected to God is so important because it is in those times where He speaks to us the most. Get creative when spending time with God! Go to the beach, go to dinner, create a space where it's just you and Him! Grab a journal, pray, dance and maybe even sing (it doesn't have to good singing! Trust me I know!) Take the time to dwell on John 15:4-5:

> *Stay joined to me, and I will stay joined to you. Just as a branch cannot produce fruit unless it stays joined to the vine, you cannot produce fruit unless you stay joined to me. I am the vine, and you are the branches. If you stay joined to me, and I stay joined to you, then you will produce lots of fruit. But you cannot do anything without me.*

_____

_____

CHAPTER 8: **IT COMES WITH THE TERRITORY**

Each person has their own load. Some may be lighter than others, some may be heavy. Either way, we must all carry our own because we have certain muscles to strengthen in order to run the race we've been assigned. When we get to the point of fatigue and weariness, we are tempted to take off our load; saying to ourselves that we have had enough and that we want out, or that we can very much do without it. STOP RIGHT THERE! Trust me, I hear you, *Courtney, you don't know what I've been through or have to face from day to day, this is seriously too much for me to handle;* however if we choose to take our load off, in other words, run away from every single problem or trial that comes our way, we hurt ourselves drastically. Do body builders get stronger using the same amount of weight? No, but they gain their strength by adding more and more weight to their training regimen.

You see, dear heart, yes you may experience pain and struggles that seem just so unbearable that you can barely even think about taking one more step, but that's where our great God, our ultimate source of strength steps in. What if we thought of our troubles as a help not a hindrance? A step up and not a smack down, a helping hand and not a thieving one. Our troubles are designed to help strengthen the muscles needed to carry the load and weight of our purpose. Let's be real for a minute. Who likes to work out and lift weights? I sure don't! I HATE working out mainly because of the pain and discomfort I know that I'm going to feel. I'm still working on this, pray for me! A couple of friends and I recently purchased bicycles to change up our workout routine. I was a little nervous at first because I hadn't ridden in years. They say that you never forget how to ride a bike; though I found this to be true, I discovered another harsh reality: it hurt so bad! My legs were hurting. I was out of breath, and I won't even talk about how uncomfortable the seat was! I couldn't even make it around the neighborhood without getting off and pushing my bike all the way back home. I was discouraged because I couldn't keep up with everyone and that I was way too slow. I gave up in my mind and I accepted defeat. After the workout was over, one of my friends pulled me aside. I thought he was going to cheer me up and tell me that everything was going to be okay, but to my surprise, he didn't. He told me that riding my bike was how I've been living my life; once

CHAPTER 8: IT COMES WITH THE TERRITORY

it got hard I gave up. I need to keep pushing at my own pace and overtime I will get stronger. He told me that I couldn't stop because things got a little uncomfortable. Though exercising hurts, it's strengthening me day by day, and I can do more and feel better about myself, not to mention that I have more energy throughout the day.

I said all that to say this: your troubles are like working out, nobody likes to do it, but it is necessary for your growth and purpose. Certain situations develop certain muscles needed to sustain weight of your calling. Not only do you have to work out, you have to stretch. Talk about discomfort! But imagine how much stronger and flexible you will be. You'll be able to bend and roll with the punches of life. You'll be able to go through the storm with a smile, and not only that, you'll be able to strengthen others. What you may perceive to be despair is actually the gateway to someone else's deliverance. Think about that for a moment. Those crazy times that you may go through, those heartaches, those break ups, that sickness, that stronghold, could help someone else. You see, dear heart, I've said it before and I will say it again, the things you go through in this life are not just for you.

Mia went through the training and proper preparation in order to take her place as queen, however when the time came, she faced opposition from all sides. There were people trying to tell her who she should be and how she should become who she was destined to be. There were people even trying to sabotage her path in becoming queen. Opposition often comes at the brink of manifestation. Though situations arise, whose report will you choose to believe? That bank account that's at zero right now? That teacher that says there is absolutely no way to pass? That doctor that has given up hope? That husband/wife, boyfriend/girlfriend, friend or family member who thinks that you won't make it and that you will not amount to anything? Or will you choose to believe the God who supplies all of your needs, the God who makes ways out of no ways, the God who raised people from the dead, and the God who fearfully and wonderfully made you and has amazing plans for your life? The choice is yours. Though situations may arise, though it may look absolutely bleak and hopeless, I implore you dear reader to stick to the original plan. Hold on to the promise and the call that God has called you to. Hard times will eventually bring forth harvest times if you do not give up.

PART 3: WALKING IN PURPOSE WITH CONFIDENCE

CHAPTER 9: **STAYING HYDRATED**

I keep saying that God has a funny way of teaching us things, and some of those lessons can be long, hard, and just plain cruel at times. A few years ago, I was driving home from a long day at work, and suddenly I felt nothing but hot air coming out of my vents. I'm thinking to myself: *great, if it's not one thing, it's another.* Now for those who have never been to Florida, it's hot…year round. It is hot, extremely humid and sticky, and not having AC in the car is just not right. For the record, I was already experiencing a lot of stress, depression and anxiety with my job. I hardly had any time to take care of myself, and I was very tired. One day, I asked God how could I continue pressing on if I am physically, mentally, and spiritually exhausted? Trust me, I was past exhausted, if there was a word that described the point past exhaustion, I was there. One morning I noticed that my car's AC goes out during the hottest month of the year. A couple of days later I took Fiona, my car that my parents got me for my high school graduation, to get serviced. Thinking to myself that she only needed minor repairs, I received the diagnoses. My entire AC needed to be replaced, and it would take over $3,000 to fix it. My heart sank to the pit of my stomach. I could barely breathe, let alone move out of my chair. So many thoughts were flying across my mind: how am I supposed to drive with absolutely no air in 100 degree weather? I was a social worker at the time and I dealt with kids for most of my day. I wore so many hats, and chauffeur just so happened to be one of them. With no air and intense heat, transporting my kids would be just plain cruel. The first couple of days of driving with no air were next to impossible. It was hot, I was sweaty, and just plain mad. One day, I was driving and I suddenly felt dizzy. My throat was dry and I could barely see. I quickly pulled into a nearby fast food place and asked for two bottles of ice cold water. As I drank the first bottle of water, I felt some of my strength come back. By the time I was halfway finished with the second bottle, I was feeling like a champ, and I got into my car, I didn't even notice the heat anymore. I was cool and I was hydrated and got to my destination in a breeze.

 I say all that to go back to the question that I asked God before all of this happened. *What do you do when you are too tired to keep pressing?* As soon as I got out of the car, it hit me like a ton of bricks. In order to

CHAPTER 9: STAYING HYDRATED

keep from getting physically, mentally, and spiritually exhausted, we must stay hydrated and replenished. In this life, especially if you are going to walk in your purpose with confidence, there are going to be seasons where you're going to get tired and it's going to feel as if you have no more gas in your tank, but take heart and know that there is indeed hope and a solution! With our physical man, we need water to stay hydrated. Our mental man needs positive thinking and reinforcement, and most importantly, our spirit man needs Living Water and Daily Bread, which is God alone. We will not be able to fully walk in the purpose God has placed inside of us if we are not constantly connected to our life-giving source. It's so crucial. Let's take a quick look at John 15:16:

> ***I am the vine; you are the branches. If you remain in me and I in you, you will bear much fruit; apart from me you can do nothing.***

We constantly need to stay connected to Jesus to function. Think about it, just as we charge our phones and other devices, we must stay plugged in to God. Can you imagine life without your charger? I know I can't. You wouldn't be able to charge anything and all would be lost once your phone dies; that means no more texting and no more social media. Without your charger, your phone will have no life and no use at all, and it is the same for us. Without a true relationship with God and without spending time with Him through prayer and reading His Word, we have no life and we would be unable to fulfill our purpose.

An empty vessel is only as good as its use. Take a drinking glass for example. A drinking glass is not a glass if it is used to hold plants, candy or other objects. The drinking cup will not be serving in its full purpose if it is filled with things that are unnecessary and irrelevant to its use. It is when that glass is filled with the right substance: water, juice, etc. that it is able to be fully used to its full capacity. Like us, we cannot be used to our fullest ability if we are filled with unnecessary things, people, secrets, and dare I say it, sin. It is that moment when we humble ourselves and allow God to fill us with His fresh and living water that we are able to be fully used and able to effectively walk in our purpose.

CHAPTER 10: **THE PRICE OF PURPOSE**

Purpose is birthed through process; that is why we can't give up. It always comes with a price. The anointing, that power God gives us to complete the work that He calls us to must cost us something, and for followers of Christ, that means it costs us everything. For me, it costed me years of rejection, verbal and mental abuse, and many years of isolation and even betrayal from the ones I thought had my back. I realized that I didn't go through those things because God didn't love me, but because He wanted my full dependence to be in Him alone. I couldn't start the ministry God placed in me right away. There had to be a process of stripping and pruning. I still had nastiness in my heart that needed to come out. I still compared myself, I was still jealous of others, I was bitter, I didn't love myself, and most importantly, my relationship with God was nowhere near where it needed to be. My heart wasn't fully surrendered to God. There were still some areas in my life that *I* wanted control over.

I wanted to find my husband. *I* wanted to be "promoted" and be "famous" in ministry. **I, I, I**....talk about being selfish! I needed to learn how to chase after Him wholeheartedly and to intercede for others and sit at His feet. I needed to find true contentment in Him. I needed to understand that my worth didn't come from a guy, my friends, a title or even ministry, my worth came from Him and Him alone. Before God releases us to walk in what He has for us, there is a stripping/pruning process that we must go through. This is a time where God strips our hearts of all those things that aren't like Him. It's also in this time where the enemy tries to attack us the most. I went through a season where God was pruning and checking me every single day. I felt like it was going to last forever. It was in that time where I felt the enemy in my ear the most, often telling me that I would never survive this season and that God forgot about me and left me here to die. At first it was hard because in one ear, I had the Holy Spirit encouraging me but in the other, I heard the enemy loud and clear. I wanted to give up and tell God if I had to go through all of that, it wasn't worth it. I felt like it wasn't worth my sanity. It wasn't worth losing sleep over and stressing to the point of getting migraines and being sick to my stomach every time a situation didn't go my way. Overtime, God showed me that if I was being attacked in this way, I was in good company. Even Jesus went through a season of testing and temptation before He started His ministry. Let's take a look at Matthew 4:1-11:

> *Then Jesus was led by the Spirit into the wilderness to be tempted by the devil. 2 After fasting forty days and forty nights, he was hungry. 3 The tempter came to him and said, "If you are the Son of God, tell these stones to become bread."*
>
> *4 Jesus answered, "It is written: 'Man shall not live on bread alone, but on every word that comes from the mouth of God."*
>
> *5 Then the devil took him to the holy city and had him stand on the highest point of the temple. 6 "If you are the Son of God," he said, "throw yourself down. For it is written:*
>
> *"'He will command his angels concerning you, and they will lift you up in their hands, so that you will not strike your foot against a stone."*
>
> *7 Jesus answered him, "It is also written: 'Do not put the Lord your God to the test.'"*
>
> *8 Again, the devil took him to a very high mountain and showed him all the kingdoms of the world and their splendor. 9 "All this I will give you," he said, "if you will bow down and worship me."*
>
> *10 Jesus said to him, "Away from me, Satan! For it is written: 'Worship the Lord your God, and serve him only.'*
>
> *11 Then the devil left him, and angels came and attended him.*

Can you believe that? The enemy completely tried Jesus! Instead of falling for the enemy's scheme, Jesus overcame him by proclaiming the Word. Every time the enemy had something to say, Jesus would throw the Word back in his face. We must do the same thing. It's so important to be grounded and rooted in the Word of God, so when a situation, attack or a test pops up, we can instantly remember what the Bible says about it and speak against what is trying to trip us up. There was a time where the enemy's lies were so loud in my ear, and it got to the point where I started to believe them and it affected the way I maneuvered in my relationships. The enemy's lies became my truth and my reality. God showed me that He was teaching me how to fight. He led me to make notecards with scriptures that spoke against what the enemy was saying to me. Every time I would hear the lie, I would combat it with the truth. Overtime I had those scriptures memorized and used them in my daily prayers. I believe it was in that season that God was teaching me warfare because before that moment, I didn't know how to fight. I would just let the enemy hit me, but now, I'm stronger and so much better. Do the lies still try to come? Absolutely, but I know how to deal with it and have victory over it now. When we understand the cost of our anointing, we value it a little more. We'll be able to understand why we had to go through something. I can look back on certain situations and just smile and tell God thank you. I know that I've faced rejection and have been overlooked so many times in my life, but now I know that it wasn't because God didn't love me, He was hiding me from people and things that could take advantage of me and steer me off track. I know I really wanted to be with that guy in more ways than one and it felt like no one saw me and wanted to pursue me, but in actuality it was God shielding me. He knew what I wanted but because of the anointing He had placed inside of me, He needed to keep me pure and free from contamination. He knew there would be people out there that I would have to minister to concerning purity and virtue. He saw the long run. He saw farther than my natural eyes could see and He knew way more than my finite mind could even begin to comprehend, so I had to trust Him. I understood why I had to go through certain things, I felt more empowered to do the thing God called me to do. In this process, we have to remember who we are and remember the promise God has spoken over us. When the enemy is trying to run us down, we must run to Jesus, fall on our face and pursue His presence at all costs. Giving into the enemy's lies isn't worth what God wants to do through you once He releases you.

CHAPTER 11: **THE WAITING GAME**

Sometimes God requires us to wait for the things He's promised us. The question is, what are we doing in the meantime? We must be active participants for our purpose to be birthed. God is a gentlemen, He's not going to force you to do something you don't want to do. We can't ask God to lead us and guide our footsteps if we don't pick up our feet and walk! Our process is a two way street! Let's be real, that in between time knowing what God's going to do and actually seeing it fulfilled can be brutal, but it's awesome to know that we don't have to be mean in our meantime! Now, I want you to think about this: what are you doing in your meantime?

We have to be faithful in the things God has placed on our plates before He gives us more. Think about dinner time when you were a kid. Remember those times where you had to sit there at the table until you ate everything on your plate?

I hated those moments!!! I didn't want to eat

that stuff! I was so focused on digging into that sweet potato pie that just got out of the oven. Forget what is on my plate, give me the pie!! The same goes for us. Think about it; yes, God gave you this grand vision for your life. You may be called to preach, write books, or start an organization or a business, but what has God told you to do right now? Are there some tests that you still need to pass? You may be called to help people, but are you still mean and roll your eyes at those who may get on your nerves? Sure, you're called to start a business but have you learned how to budget and manage your money? What about your time? (I'm still working on this one ya'll) Have I always passed this test? Ha! Yeah, right. I know God has called me to help His people, but there were times where I was bitter and jealous. Sometimes I would get mad at God because I felt like everyone else's gifts were noticed and that I was just in the background. I felt that other people always got the shot when I'm over here working my butt off behind the scenes and no one would notice.

There was a season where I thought it was finally time to walk in a position I thought God was calling me to. I was just so sure that it was time. I was faithful. I passed so many tests and the timing just seemed to perfect to me; only to find out that I was completely wrong and someone else was chosen. I got so angry and offended at God. I couldn't sleep, I could barely

CHAPTER 11: THE WAITING GAME

think and all I could say to God was what the heck? Then, He really convicted me. I came to realize that I wasn't really ready. There were some things in my heart that I still needed to work out. I was too dependent on people's approval. If I were to step into that position at that time, I would have crumbled under the pressure. I look back and laugh now because God showed me that I wasn't even supposed to have that position in the first place. I said all that to say this: don't neglect the process. Sure, there are some things in your heart that you want to do. Sure, you're asking God for a spouse that will love and cherish you. Sure, you may want that promotion, but are you truly ready for it? Is your heart in the right place? Is there bitterness, pride, resentment or perversion in your heart that you haven't worked out yet? I challenge you to let God in and let Him perfect you. Don't worry, those visions and desires will still be there, but as you allow the Lord to work in your heart and perfect everything concerning you, those desires and visions will ultimately be His and you'll be led by Him in order to see them fulfilled! Habakkuk 2:3 tells that we must wait for the vision to come to past and it will come without delay. Want to know a secret? There is no delay when it comes to God! His timing and our timing don't even compare.

Be encouraged and know that God's timing

concerning us is absolutely perfect! In those waiting times we have to trust with all of our heart that God's intentions and plans for us are good and we must hope and expect that His perfect will WILL be done in His perfect timing. If you're in a season of waiting, take heart. God sees you, He knows your heart. He's wanting you to fully rely on Him. Matthew 6:33 tells us that if we seek Him and His way of doing things then everything else will line up. Waiting is hard, but God is good, and He's so faithful, continue to cling to Him and you can't go wrong.

CHAPTER 12: **CHANGE BEGINS WITH YOU!**

Before we are able to reach others, we must first examine ourselves. We cannot touch people with dirty hands full of germy sin. This contact will cause others to be infected, thus eventually causing a spiritual epidemic where many people find themselves spiritually unhealthy and on the brink of death. We must constantly ask God to search us and to find and uproot anything that is not like Him. The closer we get to the Light, the more we see ourselves and those spots and blemishes that aren't like Him. I remember on one occasion God whooped the mess out of me. I thought I was closer to Him than I actually was. Granted I was still serving in ministry, trying to help those around me, but all the while my heart was still jacked up. One of my favorite worship songs is "More" by Lawrence Flowers and Intercession. The song is a conversation with God saying that we will give Him more of our life, time, heart, etc. One morning during my quiet time, the Lord said to me. "Courtney, you say you're giving me more, when really you aren't. You doing all of these things don't please me, what pleases me is you giving me your whole heart."

I used to get so discouraged in those seasons where God would show me things that I never knew that were there and were just plain ugly. I've gone through many seasons of my life where I would ask God to show me my heart's condition and what it really looked like, and just when I thought I was further along than I was, God would call me out and immediately humble me. I can remember a time where I was so obsessed with the way I looked, how I dressed, how I carried myself and how I came off to others that it completely blinded me from what I was really supposed to be doing. I was so busy trying to portray an image of this perfect and wholesome girl that I had cooked up in my head that I completely forgot what was important. I was so obsessed with making sure I looked just right so that I can catch some man's eye and get tons of compliments so that I could fill this nasty void that I had deep down inside. Forget the fact that God could have filled that void all along, I still wanted attention. I still wanted that title. I still wanted to be seen because I was so tired of being in the background; I thought it was my time to shine. I still wanted to compare myself to this person and that person and find some kind of false fulfillment when I felt like I one-upped them. I looked in the mirror one morning getting ready to go out and I hardly even recognized myself. I clearly heard God say "This isn't who I've created you to be. You've become so preoccupied with making yourself look good on the outside when your heart has been jacked up all this time. Those people and those things are never going to fulfill you because only I can do that." Talk about a wakeup call! God really made me take a good look at myself that day. I encourage you, take a good look at yourself; not just with your physical eyes, but really look into your spiritual mirror. What do you see? Is there a greed or pride issue that's hindering you from truly fulfilling what God has called you to do? Is it lust? Fear? Rebellion? What is it? Ask God to reveal to you those things that aren't like Him so that He can mold you and make you into the person He's designed you to be all along. Those seasons of seeing who I really was hurt, but I knew that the exposure was necessary in order to fully move forward in Christ. Romans 12:3 tells us to not think of ourselves highly than we are, but rather have a humble and realistic perspective of where we truly are. So the question is, what do you do when God shows you who you really are? First, you must thank Him. Thank Him for loving you enough not to leave you where you are. God wants to take us from faith to faith, and from glory to glory. We must always be seeking more in our relationship with God. We must repent. Repent and turn away from those things, those thoughts, feelings and tendencies that we were unaware of, even the things we blatantly knew about and acted on.

Psalm 37:4 tells us that if we delight ourselves in God, meaning if we seek to get to know Him more and live for Him wholeheartedly, then He will give us the desires of our heart. Now, let me be clear. That doesn't necessarily mean that if we follow God then He's going to give us every single thing that we want. God's not a genie, and He doesn't work like that. What this means is that when we fully surrender our will to His, He is able to fill us with everything that He wants for us. When we desire and pursue God, we will then develop a desire for the things of Him and what He wants for us. That may mean that you may not get that house, that car, that job, that husband/wife, that title or promotion that you have been wanting for years. If it's His will for you to have those things, then He will certainly give them to you! I always encourage myself by saying "God always has my best interest at heart." No matter how hard the change might be, no matter who or what you may have to give up in the long run, just trust Him enough and know that He always has your best interest at heart.

CHAPTER 13: **PORTION CONTROL: THE DANGER OF COMPARISON**

We all have our days where we think to ourselves, we're not as pretty or as good looking as others or we're not as smart or talented. Regarding purpose, we may think that we're not as anointed as others, so what's the point of even getting out there?

Can I be honest with you? I struggled with comparison for years. <u>Often</u> I would find myself thinking that I wasn't as smart, pretty, talented, skinny as other people were. When I entered into ministry comparing became almost second nature to me. I would duck out of things because I thought that someone else could do it better. I wouldn't want to pray for other people because I felt like I wasn't anointed enough to call down heaven and lay people out. I wouldn't want to even speak or teach because I felt that I wasn't strong enough or as outgoing and relatable as other people were. It even got to the point where I didn't even want to participate in worship because it wasn't like everyone else's.

Comparison and jealousy can make you do some crazy things. You know that saying, "The grass isn't always greener on the other side?" Ok seriously, who came up with that? Who seriously had all the time in the world to step away from their own lawn to observe somebody else's and come to that conclusion? I say that instead of worrying about what everyone else is doing, we should focus on our own lawn and make it pretty. Plant your favorite flowers. Grow some yummy watermelon. Focus on YOUR stuff.

We have to use what we've been given to our advantage and not waste time wishing that we had what someone else had. You don't know what they went through to get those things. They could have gone through hell and back just to get where they are today. Are you really willing to go through their process and completely abandon your own? We each have to make use of the cards that we've been dealt. Each of us have been dealt a different hand.

Like I said before, comparison can consume you and make you do some crazy things. Let's take the story of Cain and Abel in Genesis 4, for example. Cain and Abel were brothers. Abel worked as a shepherd and Cain cultivated the ground. When it was time to bring an offering to the Lord Abel brought his best, while Cain only brought some of his crops as a sacrifice and didn't have the right heart. Long story short, the Lord accepted Abel's offering but not Cain's. Cain became angry and jealous, but in the midst of that, God told him how to make it right. Sadly, Cain's anger and jealousy got the best of him and he ended up killing his brother and losing everything as a punishment. Had Cain made his offering right when God asked him to, he would have been blessed. Since he was so consumed with comparing himself to Abel's offering, Cain lost everything. We have to think of ourselves the same way.

Comparison and jealously makes us veer off track from what God has for us. When we're so busy focusing on someone else's lawn, ours become neglected and of no use. Picture it. Each of your neighbors have been assigned to grow some type of crop on their lawn in order to sell at the local market. Let's just say you were assigned to plant watermelon in your yard (I love watermelon, can you tell?), but you didn't want to grow watermelon, you wanted strawberries. Everyone loves strawberries. You get so focused on the neighbor who was assigned to produce strawberries that you don't even put in the work on your own assignment. Your lawn becomes dry because you haven't watered and fertilized it and now your lawn has become so brittle to the point where the ground can't even produce a harvest. Just think, those people who really loved watermelon won't be able to purchase any because you were so focused on the neighbor who had the assignment/purpose/gift that you wanted.

When we compare, we get so focused on what others are doing that we lose sight of what God has placed inside of us. We forget the fact that He has made each and every one of us unique and that we have a purpose that only we can fulfill, and that's where the enemy wants us. He wants us to be stuck and stagnant. The enemy doesn't want us focused on the will of God for our lives. The enemy doesn't want us to have authentic relationship with God because then we'll discover who we are. We'll understand that what God placed inside of us will be put to good use.

When you get tempted to compare yourself to others in any way, remember that Christ is your focus. When it comes to our walks with God, we can't look to the right, or to the left, but straight ahead to where He wants us. Galatians 6:4 tells that if we focus on our own work, we will receive a job well done from Him and we won't even have to worry about what other people are doing. Looking back to my knee injury, I would get so worked up and so consumed on what others were doing and what they could and what I couldn't that I completely lost sight of the work God wanted to do through me in that particular season. It took some

CHAPTER 13: PORTION CONTROL: THE DANGER OF COMPARISON

serious checking and some serious testing to snap me back. I look back on it now and smile. I absolutely love my portion and wouldn't trade it for anything in the world.

During that time I was able to sit at the feet of Jesus for hours without having to worry about being at this place or attending that meeting or helping out at that event. I was able to rest when I needed to and didn't have to worry about having time for myself and getting things done. When I was tempted to compare myself to certain people, it became my first instinct to pray for them, and now it's become a habit for me. I prayed that God would continue to strengthen them for the tasks they are assigned to. I would pray that He would meet their needs and to give them rest. I would pray that they wouldn't grow weary in their well doing and that they would glorify God in all that they did. I came to realize that this life isn't about me and that God had me right where He needed me, and that is when I regained my focus. Just remember, when you are tempted to look to your left or your right, look straight ahead to Christ.

CHAPTER 14: **FEAR DELAYS YOUR FUTURE**

The quicker we get over ourselves, the quicker we can walk in our purpose. Seriously, as we continue to hide behind our masks and believe the enemy's lies that we can never be that minister, that speaker, that author that God has called us to be, there is a world that is dying. One of the biggest lessons that I have learned is that this life is more than about me. My fears and my insecurities got me nowhere. It was when I finally got over myself that I was able to do what I needed to do effectively. I used to detest speaking. I would get so nervous and just stutter away. I talk to my friends whom I also serve in ministry with about this subject all the time. We would always joke and say that if someone were to initially tell us that we had to speak to people as a part of our calling, we would have checked out a long time ago. I admit, I still get a bit nervous at times. My hands sweat and I just feel like running away, thinking to myself "Eh, I'm good where I'm at. I reach people when I dance and through my writings so, that should be enough, right? There's no need for them to hear me speak, besides, I have nothing interesting to say anyway." When I think about what God has called me to do, I realize that speaking is so necessary.

Fear causes us to be comfortable with where we are, thus causing us to never progress. If you look in Exodus 3 and 4, you'll see that Moses, the great leader and prophet who parted the Red Sea and led his people to freedom even stuttered. He didn't even think he could speak to Pharaoh let alone save millions of people, but he gave his will, his insecurities and fear over to the Lord and eventually his purpose was fulfilled. Let me drop this off to you: your purpose is going to cause you to move out of your comfort zone; I know it did for me! A few years ago, I preached my very first sermon. Let me tell you, as soon as I was told that I would be preaching, my first instinct was to run; so many thoughts ran through my mind. "Me? Preach? I'm no preacher! I mean, I know that's what God has called me to do, but how can this happen?! What am I going to say? Oh goodness, how in the world is this going to sound?" Needless to say that I had to immediately give those thoughts over to God, and as I surrendered my assignment to Him. He gave me the words to say and exactly how to say them! I'll never forget when the service was over how so many people came up to

CHAPTER 14: FEAR DELAYS YOUR FUTURE

me and told me how blessed they were because of the sermon. How funny is it that out of all the things I could preach on, my sermon was centered around The Lion King!

We really need to get to the point where we do not care about our flaws, shortcomings, or what we think we should do or who we should be. There is a dying world out there searching everywhere for answers they are never going to get if we're too afraid to sing that song, get in front of the people, to speak to that person, or better yet, embrace who we are and go with it. I know for me, one of my biggest struggles was actually stepping out and doing what I was instructed to do. If a Sunday came and my Pastor would ask us to pray for people, I would literally shake. I didn't want to do it and I figured that other people could do it because I usually don't pray for people out in the open. I'm telling you, my mind was totally twisted!

There are some who have the most anointed voices and they can minister and captivate people through the way they speak and carry themselves. Sometimes when we are afraid of the unfamiliar or afraid of what other people may say, or whatever the reason is, we can tend to harbor those gifts. I've learned that as we harbor our gifts and our talents, we are committing spiritual manslaughter. Think about it, we have certain people that we are assigned to; some of them know Christ and some don't. There are people all over the world who are dying a slow and painful death and we are the only ones who holds the antidote to save them. When we become afraid of what others may think or become intimidated by the hard work and the process that comes with purpose, we withhold that antidote. The antidote we carry is the gift that very well could have led that person to the one true healer, Christ Jesus.

We see celebrity after celebrity, philanthropist after philanthropist doing the very thing that we were placed here for: reaching and inspiring others through the gifts given to them, but as you look closely, are the people that they are reaching being fulfilled? Are they truly being set free and delivered from that addiction or stronghold? Absolutely not! 2 Timothy 1:7 tells us that God has not given us a spirit of fear, but of POWER, LOVE and of a SOUND MIND.

It is time, dear heart, to look straight inside of yourself and say "this is who I am, I may not be the most confident person, I may not be the most popular person, I may stutter, I may not be able to sing, dance or speak like so and so can, but here I am. God has given me these gifts and I will not be afraid to use them to help save others." The world is waiting. God wants to use you, and someone needs to hear YOUR story. Revelation 12:11 tells us that we overcome by the blood of the Lamb and the word of our testimonies. Someone is in need of YOU, yes YOU. YOU are the gateway to leading someone else to their healing and restoration. YOU are the vessel that could help mend broken families and broken homes. YOU, yes, YOU are the key to unlocking another person's door to freedom, wholeness, and joy in Christ. What are you waiting for?

CHAPTER 15: DEAL OR NO DEAL? ACCEPTING THE OFFER

Discovering God's purpose for your life means NOTHING if you're not living for Him and Him alone. We must fully surrender to the God who places that purpose, that calling inside of us. Can I be honest with you? So many people are so busy trying to find this great call that God has for them but in reality, God made us for one purpose and for one purpose only, and that is to glorify Him and to have an intimate relationship with Him. Honestly, finding "purpose" isn't rocket science, all it takes is total surrender to Christ. Matthew 7:22-23 talks about people- good , bad, pastors, prophets, teachers, preachers, you name it- who are going to stand before the Lord one day and be turned away from Him. Sure they preached until their faced turned blue, sure they prayed for people, sure they were walking in their "purpose"; but God is going to tell them, "depart from me, I never knew you". God isn't concerned about us doing all these things for Him. He's concerned with having a real relationship with us. Your purpose alone isn't going to get you to Heaven, knowing Him for yourself is the key. Notice that God didn't say "depart from me because you didn't fulfill your calling," He said "depart from me because I never knew you."

When God first revealed to me what He placed me on the earth to do in order to reach His people, I was so excited! I began serving. I taught youth. I danced all around the nation, but deep down I was still empty. I was still depressed. Something was still missing. It wasn't until I began to have a relationship with God for real that I felt whole. Again, a purpose and a calling alone isn't going to get you into heaven, knowing Him will. God made us to have intimate relationship with Him which was His plan from the beginning of time. When Adam and Eve disobeyed God and ate the fruit in the book of Genesis, they lost that direct access man had with God, but take heart and know that God is calling us back. He came and lived here on earth just as we do and went through the same things we go through and died for our sins. He came and died so that we can have that direct access to Him again. He is calling us to know Him FIRST, and then He calls us to make Him known in the earth through the gifts that He has placed inside of us.

We have to come to a place where we want God for ourselves and not just the things He can give us and do for us. Granted, God calls His people to do amazing things for Him, but we have to have a true relationship with Him first; and yes, there are going to be times where you're going to have to go through things. Are you willing to accept the offer of an abundant life filled with favor, joy, and meaning even if it means that you will eventually suffer loss, heartache and loneliness? Trials will come, things happen in our lives that we do not necessarily agree with, but I just want to encourage you, dear heart, that God has been there all along. If you just surrender those feelings, those people, your life to Him, He can work wonders. Your package deal is completely free of charge! It has already been paid for by Jesus Christ, who freely gave His life so that we can live for Him and with Him one day.

Our purpose is a package deal and there is a lot that comes with what God wants us to do and how He wants us to live. In order to accept that offer, we must accept God; accept God into our hearts and get to know Him for ourselves. All He wants is a "Yes". "Yes God, even though I've been through hell and high water in my life, I will still follow you". "Yes God, even though I've been hurt and abandoned by every single person in my life, I'll still trust you." "Yes God, I really don't know how to walk in purpose just yet, but I trust you enough to show me." "Yes God, I give you my life". We must get to the place where we can trust God enough to always move on our behalf. If God has shown you something, your future, things that He has called you to do, best believe that it will come to past! Philippians 1:6 tells us that He that began the work will complete it. I know most of the time, well for me anyway, I would always say how excited but nervous I am about something. Just thinking back, I was working full time, diligently serving in my church and mentoring kids; not to mention that I still had to take care of myself and make time for my family and friends. Although I knew everything that God showed me was coming to past, I couldn't help but think how it was all going to get done. I have bills to pay. I have loans. I have to eat. I have to pay my tithe. God I have to pay for this, that and the other thing how in the world do you expect me to pay for everything in the future? You may say, God, I don't know what I'm doing here, I don't even know who to talk to, better yet, I have absolutely no one to connect with. How is this really going to get done? The word tells us that the steps of a righteous man are ordained by God. Proverbs 3:5-6 tells us to trust in the Lord with all your heart and don't rely on our own understanding, in all of your ways acknowledge Him and HE will direct your paths. This means that we have to make God on the throne of EVERY aspect of our lives. We have to get to a place where we can say "God, you are Lord over my relationships. God, you are Lord over my household. God, you are Lord over my finances. God you are Lord over the dreams and visions that you have placed inside me, and now God, I ask that you guide me and lead me." Ask yourself these questions:

> ***How submitted am I to Him? Meaning have I given all of my plans and desires over to Him so that He can work them out?***

> ***Can I really handle all of this on my own?***

And the last question....

> ***Do I really know who God is?***

I say all that to say, you cannot trust a God you do not know. You wouldn't leave your child, your precious baby, in the hands of a total stranger, would you? I implore you, dear heart, to get to know Him for yourself. He is the Alpha and Omega, meaning that He knows your beginning, where you were and where you are right now. He sees and delights in every detail of your life. I encourage you to get to know this God who makes ways out of no ways. Get to know the God who is a healer and a restorer. God has placed you on this earth to draw His people back to Him. I ask that you just walk it out. Though it may seem scary, and though it may seem extremely overwhelming, just move forward. You're not going to get anywhere staying still. Trust God enough and know that even in the bad times, those times where you just wanted to end it all, those times where you just wanted to throw in the towel; it was in those moments where God was shaping you. Romans 8:28 encourages us that all things work for our good for those that love God and are called according to His purpose. Those painful moments were all a part of your package deal. Let's be real, none of us know what will come in the package deal God offers us. I sure don't, and I probably never will, but I trust the creator of the deal in the first place. Our package deals are not one size fit all, meaning that we each have a purpose that only we can do. We must get to the place where we can say that no matter what comes with my package deal, I know that God is in control, and that He will not put me in anything that I know wouldn't be beneficial to me in the long run. The deal is on the table, will you have faith enough to accept the offer?

www.ingramcontent.com/pod-product-compliance
Lightning Source LLC
Chambersburg PA
CBHW071153090426
42736CB00012B/2318